Suzi QUATRO

THROUGH MY HEART

Poetry & Reminiscences

Volume Two

newhaven
publishing

Published 2022
First Edition
NEW HAVEN PUBLISHING LTD
www.newhavenpublishingltd.com
newhavenpublishing@gmail.com

Photo Credits:
Front cover © Romero Britto
Back Cover © Andrew Whitton
Page 6 (Prologue) © James Nuttall
All others from Suzi's personal collection

Cover Design © Pete Cunliffe

newhaven
publishing

Contents

Dedication	5
Prologue	7

The Poems:

My Life	9
Damaged Goods	11
Tired Of Caring	13
Tonight, Tonight	15
Non Negotiable	17
The Wounded Warrior	19
Always and Forever	21
I Don't Want To Fight	23
Contemplation	25
Distance	27
Amnesia	29
WHY?	31
Woman On A Mission	33
Fame Or Famine	35
And The Clock Struck 12	39
Moments	41
Hindsight	43
Patterns	45
To Us!	47
Don't Forget To Remember	49
Battles Of The Wills	51
The Wake Up Call	53
Soul Mate	55
It's Time	57
Another Level	59
The Night Is My Enemy	61
Tumblin' Down	63
There Was A Little Girl	65
Destination Normal	67
The Window	69
Victory	71

Between the Beat	73
Who Would Have Thought It?	75
On The Road	77
Realities	79
Too Much Sadness	81
Power You	83
Time Has Beaten Us	85
Dark Tunnels	87
Random Thoughts, 4.15am	89
Toughen Up	91
Friendly No More	93
Christmas Catch-22	95
To Be Honest	97
Love Is...	99
Fractions	101
Judgement Day	103
Only A Bridge	105
Observations	107
Suddenly	109
Midnight Musings	111
The Poet	113
Sometimes	115
The Dilemma	117
The Victim	119
Yesterday, Today, Tomorrow	121
Odd Lines And Misdemeanors	123
Untitled	125
Amoral	127
Elephant In The Room	129
My Mom, My Heart, Forever	131
The Least Offensive	133
Born Free	135
Blood Binds, Blood Ties	137
Ode To Suzi Q	139
The Meeting	141

This book is dedicated to everyone who has shared my life in whatever form and for whatever reason they have shared it.
The road we travel is never easy.
But one thing you can guarantee,
it will have a beginning and it will have an end.
Everything else is open to interpretation.

Wishing you everything you wish yourselves.

it's a long lonely walk to get to the 'stage' of life,
and a long lonely walk back.

Prologue

There is a back story to my second poetry book.

Every famous person, (God I hate that word), has fans, famous equals fans, they go together. Sometimes if the famous person is a 'real' person, and the fan is persistent and clever, they share confidence and becomes friends, this is what happened to us.

It began with a simple email asking what some of my poems in *Through My Eyes* meant, not intrusive, just curious, which was, fine. This started a chain of trust and the communication flowed.

I decided, as I was assembling this book, to use this experience, and also to honour it. These things don't happen very often.

I have trusted my fan/friend enough to bounce most of the poems in this book off her, even before I had tweaked them, which is amazing in itself.

Was I seeking approval, was I wanting applause? Well, even if both things are true, the point is - I shared, and could have been shot down in an ambush of disapproval. I wasn't.

But, had I been, I would have respected that.

My fan/friend is clever, analytical, and compassionate with tragedies and disappointments of her own, which is where we truly connect.

She has been a perfect sounding board and I thank her for that.

And now…. Here is my book

THROUGH MY HEART

PS... She will remain anonymous!!

• at home, 1980, my mother, forever in my heart

It's so strange sometimes being one of life's gypsies and, as my mother always said, gypsy is in our bloodline - her being Hungarian.

Everything seems so transient. How many times I have woken up, wondering where the hell I am, always leaving a light on in the bathroom so at least I won't trip and break my neck on the way. This was written on a trip to Hamburg where my husband's house is.

And, as was the way with most of the poems in this poetry book number 2, written in the early hours.. 4 a.m. so it says.. and my favorite line in the poem is...

"Catholic is the reason I stand tall when I stoop".

My Life

This is my life, as I float back and forth,
Home, yet 'not' home.
A visitor is somebody else's life,
And, between them I roam.
laying here at 4 a.m., not my bedroom
Not my pictures on the wall
Not my pillows, not my bed,
NOT my life.
Which makes my mind wander and twist down dark
alley ways.
What do you remember when it is 'that' time?
The blinds on the window, one light shining across
the road,
On constantly, for no apparent reason?
I reach for the brandy.
Instagram, Facebook, whatever, I need to
communicate.
Is this my destiny, or insanity?
Please neither of you ever leave me,
Never… Never… Never.
I wonder, does anyone get me? In fact, do I get me?
My life privileged yet underprivileged.
Can they co-exist? Oh yes, they can…. and they do.
All lives leave a residue
Of tear drops and magic.
And now Morpheus calls softly, eyelids droop,
Escaping into subconscious, through that guilty
hoop.
Catholic is the reason
I stand tall when I stoop.
I will turn out the lights, eye mask in place.
Lay with my memories, lost in this space.
My life my life…who else's can it be
I lived it, I own it, with all its polarity.

And my mind wanders down those dark alleyways.

Written in what looks like a very sombre mood indeed - the date is Feb 3, 2018, so, 2 years before all of our lives changed.

By memory, I thought this one could become a song... but then when I was assembling everything for this book, I decided it was much more poignant as a short and simple verse.

Favorite line from this one: "sweet temptation all around, guess I have to burn, Guess I have to burn..

Looks like 'the devil in me' is alive and well... my halo has well and truly slipped!!!

Damaged Goods

Damaged goods
I'm on the floor
Why, oh why
Did I go back for more?

Guess I'll never learn
Guess I'll never learn
Fallen angels
Waltz through hell's door

Sweet temptation
All around
Guess I'll have to burn
Guess I'll have to burn

Guess I'll never learn.

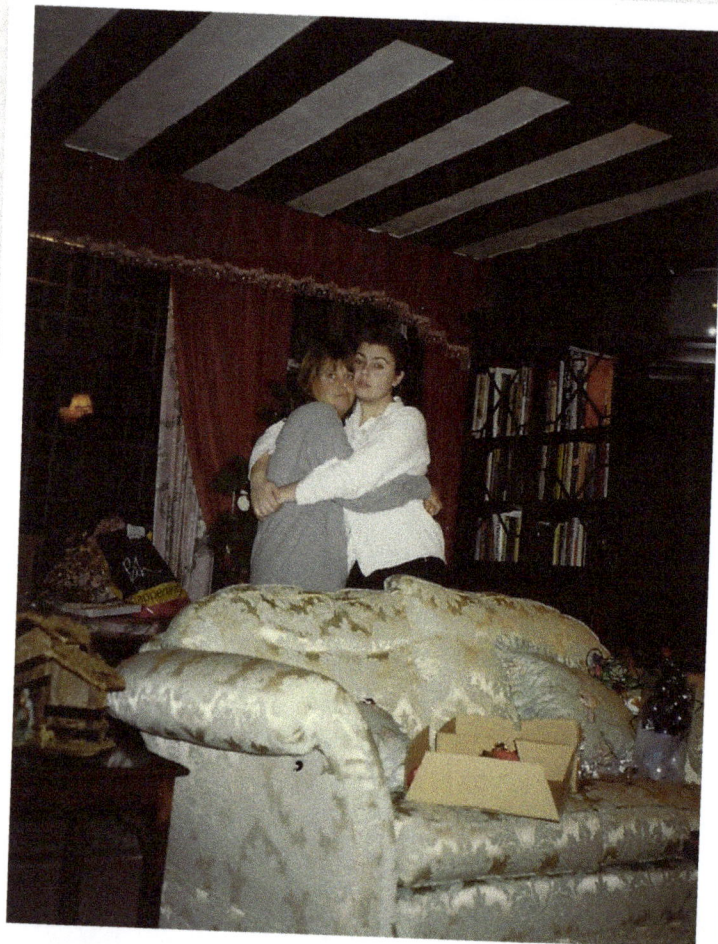

• Me and Laura...Xmas..business as usual.

Without giving too much away, because in all honesty, the reader should interpret the poem, just like any kind of art, it should speak to you.

This is obviously about somebody very close to me, who I love dearly but just can't seem to find a way forward. Me being me, I always try to do damage limitation by turning the feeling into a lyric or a poem. Its always worked, although sometimes I have to re-write it cuz it gets 'wet and blurred' ..lost in translation... that's for sure... or should that be 'lost in transition'... mmmmmmm

Tired Of Crying

You fire your arrow,
Now blunted with time.
Your truth, your version,
Well, here's mine.
I did nothing but love you,
With all my heart.
You did nothing but hate me,
And that's just the start!
I tried so damn hard
To understand your complaints,
Accusations and recriminations,
Just another coat of paint.
When reality is so easy,
Straightforward and true.
It has no agenda,
It's just me and you.
I'm so tired of hurting
I'm so tired of misconstruing
I'm so tired of burning
In your non deserving flame.
I'm so tired of excusing
The blackness in your soul.
I'm so tired of defusing
winds of hate, you blow.
I'm tired of crying
I'm tired of crying
My light is dying
And I have to let you go.

I am just so tired of crying.

And another one in my series of
'where the f.....k am I'.

This one, written in Spain at 1:12 a.m... some people
count sheep... I write poetry and wander around.

Favorite stanza in this next poem is...
"like jelly wobbly and enticing,
if you like that kind of thing"

Of course you are free to choose your own
favorite bits.

Tonight, Tonight

After midnight, darkness???
What room am I in?
Whose home, what country???
Is it mine, is it his, is it ours??
Quite a problem.
I run my fingers along the stove
Wiping the counter clean,
Putting the glasses and china in place
Breaking one or two in the process, of course!!
Plumping up pillows
That don't need plumping.
Quietly opening the sliding patio door,
Not wanting to awaken my partner.
Not wanting to answer any questions,
About my state of mind.
Now there's a phrase….my state of mind.
Like jelly... wobbly, enticing,
If you like that kind of thing.
It's a much too sweet, sickly taste,
With a bite that packs a sting.
So… shall we stop singing
this tuneless melody.
It's somehow lost its charm,
And the rest, a fallacy.
Tonight, Tonight,
God bless us all
That's all
God bless us all.

• Spanish trip 1994, Laura and Richard

Lots of things going on when this was written, including one of my good friends losing her son... so obviously I was deep down in it.

This relates and explores family relationships, which are never easy.... Never!!!. The love is there and nothing can take that away, no matter how much you may differ and argue.

But it doesn't mean you accept bad treatment without fighting back. Passive is not a word in my dictionary.. I will always fight my corner.

Non Negotiable

You're born into this world
To a family, some say you choose!
Whether you do or not,
You may win, and you may lose.
Your journey is unknowable,
But the outcome, non-negotiable.

Your sainted mother and father,
How can you see them any other way?
They push, they guide, they punish.
And rescue, when you go astray.
A future, it's undeniable,
The outcome, non-negotiable.

So, the leap from child to mother,
A new scenario, for nature to smother.
Oh, my angel, my baby, my precious one,
Yet so much to discover.
The journey is unthinkable
and the game, non-negotiable.

When did nature turn its back,
and make you fight your corner?
When did love turn to attack,
Respect into dishonour.
The scenario is unbearable.
The reality, non-negotiable.

And you sit inside your mental room.
A place of your own creation.
Like a mummy in a tomb,
Preserving what is salvageable,
Wrapped in palpitations
The pain, non-negotiable.

And if, God forbid,
the order is reversed,
and you throw dirt upon your child,
A scene that cannot be rehearsed,
The heartache inexpressible,
The end, non-negotiable

Perspective is a gift,
So, wrap carefully your perception.
No matter what angry words,
No matter the misconception
Parents, children, indefensible
Nature rules, non-negotiable.

I have always maintained, especially when it was the 'thing' to be... that I was never a woman's libber... always a 'me' libber... never thinking there was anything I could not do, if I wished to do it.

I have lived by that rule my entire life. Which makes it kind of funny that I wrote this next poem from a woman's perspective... and this from the person who has always said... 'I don't do gender'... (and I don't do gentle either!!!)... straight from the hip... that's me. If you don't want to know the answer... don't ask me the question.

And a little footnote with my 'bouncing' fan/friend, with whom I exchanged numerous emails and copies of these poems... about this next one she wrote...

"Do you blame lockdown or 'thank' lockdown for making you see 'the game' clearly?..."
and I answered...

I THANK LOCKDOWN...
EVERYTHING IS CLEAR NOW...
NO MORE ROSE COLOURED GLASSES
FOR ME.

The Wounded Warrior

The wounded warrior screams loud,
But nobody hears.
Her faith in human kindness dies,
In truth, nobody cares.

She is one lone voice,
Drowning in the abyss.
Emptiness, deep despair,
make a lethal kiss.

Fighting the good fight,
Or so it's been said,
but who makes the wrong right?
Who's alive and who is dead?

The wounded warrior bleeds,
Yet remains alive.
A knife cuts the strings,
Yet, the warrior survives.

The wounded warrior dives,
Into the blackest sea
Swimming in 'insanity'
Defending her right to fly free.

The wounded warrior soars,
and will not be contained.
Her mission is pure,
Her goal is ordained.

The wounded warrior's seeds,
Now planted in the ground
Gives rebirth and hope
Yet she remains, uncrowned.

• *Rainer and me, and this caption is, "Always and Forever".*

And in our text about this next poem...(me) " I will happily fall again and again, and I have done, for the rest of my life, and then I will take that final fall".. (she said) , Well wow, That is an intriguing sentence....

This was written at 5 minutes to midnight.. I like the way the phrases fall in this... pleasing to the eye when you read it, and pleasing to the ears when you speak it... I always like to read my poems out loud... why don't you try that. It's amazing the different interpretation it takes on when your own voice is giving my poetry a voice.

Always and Forever

Always and forever
Temporary in the best of times.
Promises, heated moments,
The scene of love crimes.
This is it, he's the one!!!
I've never felt like this before!
Always and forever,
And then… you shut the door.

Short and sweet was our song,
This lover's lament,
Always and forever,
Well… that 'was' my intent!
Never make a promise
You cannot keep.
Never set the bar
Above your lover's leap!

Always and forever,
Yes, the devil calls the tune
Always and forever,
But it all ends too soon.
Always and forever,
Words left unspoken
Always and forever
No promises… no broken.

Always and forever
Always and forever
I will leave you?, never.
Always is it… Forever?

I was flying back from Spain, got out my crossword book and found a bit of paper in the back, with words that I had started on another journey somewhere...(analogy intended).

So... the flight was spent finishing this rather good poem, if I do say so myself. I typed it out the next afternoon when I got back home.

It's a short sharp thrust, and I hope I am making my point, (pun intended), loud and clear...
OUCH!!!

I Don't Want To Fight

I don't want to even the score,
It's our scandal, behind this door
The skin off my nose
Of this juxtapose
Can't keep my light shining anymore.

Like branches of trees reach out.
Leaves bloom, then fall, in doubt.
All lessons we learn
Till we die and burn,
And the answers are lost in the blackout.

I DON'T WANT TO FIGHT
I DON'T WANT TO FIGHT
I DON'T WANT TO FIGHT,
ANYMORE.

• *Russian tour, 1989, mama and her babies taking a pit stop.*

It's amazing how consistent the times are... this next one was written at 12:07 a.m.

Something must come flying in, in the midnight hours. Me being me... I cannot rest until its on paper. Not a lot to add to this next one... it's self explanatory... favorite line... the last one...

"the little girl sings her song, whistling down the sidewalk of her life"

Contemplation

Finding my way through the mire,
Broken dreams and symphonies
I heard, yes, and I sang its song,
A need to be, I was young,
still creating my memories.
Our mom, ruling our world,
A fist of iron, yet her mind, black and white.
Our dad, earning the crust
Now his dust scatters in flight.
I follow their rules
Lessons I have learned,
Their wisdom like jewels, shine bright,
This right to question, I've earned.
Yes, contemplation is sacred
when admitting defeat.
Love versus hatred,
Opposites, yet complete.
We don't write the story,
We don't play the part,
Our movie was written
Our birth was the start.
Contemplation is sacred
My thoughts run wild,
I accept this adult
But I 'still' hug the child.
Melancholy I may be,
As I linger awhile
On the edge of what should be
Is the hint of a smile.
Consideration, acceptance
Wish upon a star.
Life is the message
Que sera sera

The little girl sings her song,
Whistling down the sidewalk of her life.

Written September 4, 2021 ...

I emailed my fan/friend (bet you're all dying to know who this is eh!... well my pen may be mighty, but my lips are sealed). I emailed her along with this offering, "Okay.. told you one was coming.. it's after 1 a.m... I could not stop this... had to keep going until it was correct... it is another 'wow'... there are no questions to ask... it is self explanatory... enjoy... now finally, going to sleep... very happy with this one... dark though it may be."

And there you have a real window into this particular artistic mind...
make of it what you will

Distance

Distance, is it mental or physical?
Is it emotional, or just geographical?
A happy oasis, of alone time,
Or a prison of the worst kind?
Distance, to another bed?
For sleep's sake.
Treason, to behead, for peace's sake.
Once intimate, now forced and cold,
Love's dichotomy grabs hold,
It's a sad sign of a bad time.
Distance, a silent retreat
Pulling up covers, between the sheets.
Can you rewind time, is it still close, warm?
Or stale and old, like those lies on your lips.
Oh, the tales, they've told!
Distance, a sea of regret,
A river of heartache,
Your mind can't forget.
The sorrow of heartache, the edge of reason
The road to mistakes, a rhyme for all seasons.
Distance? Time for a jailbreak?
What is far, what is close,
What is the difference.
What lurks below, twixt male and feline
Can we close the gap, somehow overlap?
To a love bind?
Distance… Distance… Distance…
We WILL find a way… ever the optimist

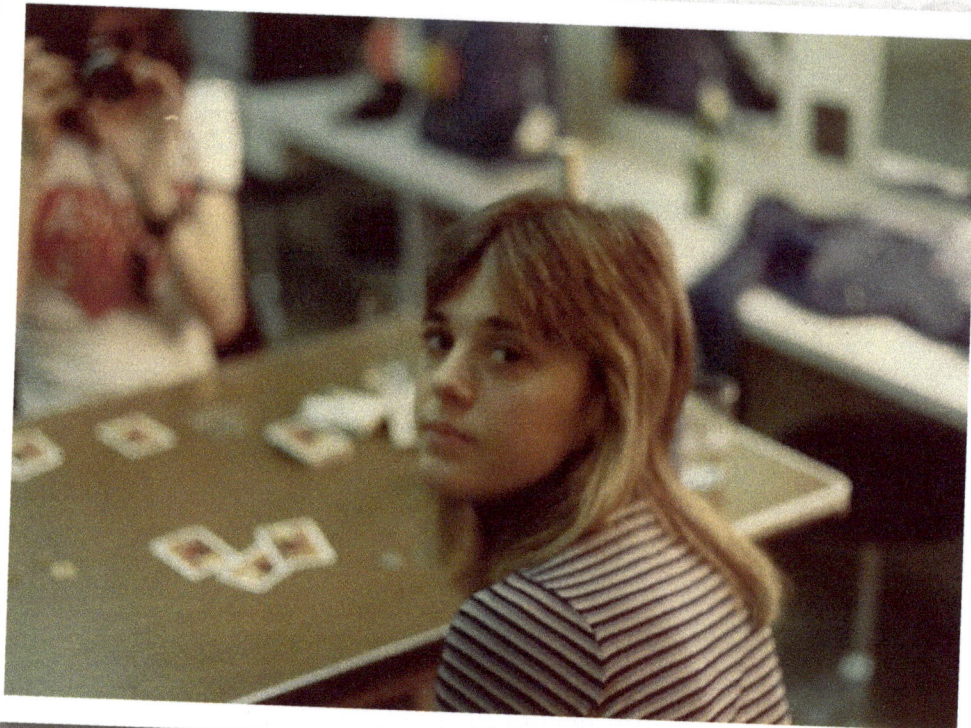

• *On tour somewhere, playing another card game in another dressing room... so.. did I win?*

These next two poems kind of made this process of writing, sending, waiting for feedback, answering questions, etc... come together in my head... I wrote "I guess you have become my proof reader, and it kind of makes sense considering the 'email' book I have in my briefcase. Maybe this was the reason for all of that, to get to this! It is nice to have a person to bounce off of , who understands me, and, questions me... good stuff. Hope you are enjoying the process, and now I will answer your comments. I have been pointing out my favorite stanzas so far... here is. 'hers' from the next poem "the inability to stay awake in your life"

Amnesia

What causes this phenomenon?
Is it the inability to sleep?
Or the inability to stay awake in your life?
What a conundrum
You climb the stairs to slumber,
Slowly, step by step, carefully,
Shedding the day's problems,
Yet, each step wakes you up to today's problems.
Damn it…. No escape.
And so I sit, computer on my lap.
Pondering my emotional abyss.
What shall I do?
Who shall I talk to?
Who can help me?
… can anyone help me?

And the answer is NO… I can only help myself.
If that's true, boy oh boy am I in trouble.

This word amnesia, what does it mean?
To forget, to forget, to what????
Whoops… I forgot.
And, as I am waiting for the angel of sleep
To sprinkle grains of release in my eyes,
I know in my heart,
That I have reached a crossroad.
No sea, no ocean, no bridge,
No emotion.
I am .... ALONE.
Amnesia,
what a nice word to blame your sorrows on.
Goodnight.

On to the next poem...

she asked "I love both of them and already read them several times.. Question: are 'Why' and "Amnesia", coming from the same train of thought (i.e. written on the same day or night....so related in emotional content) or are they completely separate?"

I answered, "same train of thought, I think lockdown has had a huge effect on me.. always knew I was self-sufficient but didn't realize how self-sufficient I am ... I have found absolute strength inside and out to survive whatever this life throws at me... and...
the strength to throw it back."

WHY?

Isolated incidences,
Late at night,
Once fed with drink
Now constantly alight.
Dialogue in movies,
Piercing my heart
Used to feel distant,
Now it blows me apart.
WHY?
A need to be loved,
a need to be needed.
If justice means judgement,
And truth is deleted,
If lost is afraid
yet wisdom shines bright
can you keep fighting the good fight?
with no end in sight?
WHY?
If you speak sweetly,
And peace is your name
Will you whisper gently
And win the game?
This remote control
 To pick the channel you choose.
Switching fact to fiction
Who cares, whatcha got to loose?
WHY?
Why why why,
Do any of us really understand
Die, die die,
Because fate, plays your hand
And the question is
WHY????
And for that… there is no answer.

• *1979/80, my beloved red BC Rich... still have it.*

Interesting that in these emails concerning the next poem, the subject matter says:

(trust is the word)... indeed... we both agree... up in 'our' top 3 of my work. I like her comments on this next offering very much –
"although loneliness has been alluded to in quite a few of your lyrics/poems, I feel that "woman on a mission" is the natural continuation of "solitude"... another poem that I personally love, written in different circumstances and separated by decades, but that space... that 'unfillable' void is still there"

Very well said, fan/friend.

Woman On A Mission

There was always an aloneness
In the fabric of 'her' time.
An awareness that she was,
One step out of time.
The one, left behind.

Too much heart, made her eyes stream
Deep with understanding,
Beyond what is visible
With knowledge
Beyond what is knowable.

True child of the universe,
In the play called 'life',
Reaping the benefits, yet,
Still suffering strife.
Words should connect,
Not cut, life a knife.

A woman of vision, she sees no façade,
A woman of integrity,
No need for charades.
A woman of vision.
A woman on a mission.

Always an aloneness
In the fabric of 'her' time.

And so on we go... into the next one, which is the longest in the book, because it's a situation I have lived with since becoming (here's that word again) 'famous'... (must find an alternative... and to all you smart asses out there, 'not' famous is not the answer!!)

This one 'had' to be written, I was really affected by the situation, went back to the house, locked myself in a room and let it all fly out... or vomit out which is a better adjective.

Our correspondence on this would make a book all on its own... so... too lengthy to repeat here... and anyway... the poem speaks for itself. Handwriting on the front from my fan/friend, "I think that our conversation on this poem needs to read in its entirety because not a lot of stuff makes me angry, but this poem did."

And for me, the poet, nothing pleases me more than getting a reaction. It means my words were heard and understood. Mission complete. Amen to that.

Fame or Famine

Today, she sat at a small café, a little make-up on.
By special request.
Look good, she was told. I want to be proud of you, she was told.
She did... he was.

She wore her best behaviour,
charming and gracious.
Ready to be whatever was required.
"Some people want to meet you",
So, she prepared to be 'that' person, 'those' people, wished to meet.
And she sat... and sat... and sat... and sat... and... sat.

Gazing face to face, listening, to a foreign language,
Trying to find space to speak, to join in.
And each time she wedged a few words in,
She was shot down in flames of disinterest.
Monologues and memories, people she did not know
People she could not understand or enjoy,
People she did not 'want' to understand or enjoy.
This was not her language; these were not her memories.

The famous person sat at the table, ignored
Nobody is comfortable with that, famous or not!

FAME OR FAMINE (continued)

She would have preferred to be invisible, to not be there
It was raining and the parade passed her by.
Hahaha… talktalktalk… blahblahblah… nothing was said.
At least, nothing anyone would remember.
Even not understanding the language, she understood that!!

She was fucking miserable.

To the toilet several times,
Glancing around the room, looking at the tables,
Trying to find 'friendly' somewhere,
so she could warm her cold shoulder,
The direct result of too many cold shoulders, that afternoon.

Wandering aimlessly around, ambling into the garden,
Trying to find a reason, any reason to 'not' go back
To the table of nothingness, to be ignored… Again!
A true communicator, about anything at all, not choosy
Able to converse on any subject, articulately
Today this was denied, and this killed that 'something' inside.
Yet it awakened in her, the killer instinct, which sharpened her mind
Into determined spikes of refusal.
Refusal to 'never' accept this, ever again.
Fame is a strange animal, she survived it many years, she survives it still

FAME OR FAMINE (conclusion)

Her mind still boggles, because she knows she has not changed.
She knows the world has changed around her.
one good thing about getting older,
The bullshit becomes clear and unbearable.
This should not have happened, and cliché though it may be,
 life is too damn short.

Today, nobody cared,
Today nobody talked to her
Today nobody wished to meet her
Today she was unseen.
What a waste of precious time
Time she could never retrieve.
Some patterns need to be broken,
Need to be broken
Need to be broken.

SNAP!!!! JOB DONE!!!

Pause......

Hey, she said to an old friend,
wanna buy me a drink and have a conversation sometime?

• 1980, Cinderella did go to the ball after all!!

Very quirky poem this next one... and the fan/friend did question where the hell it came from?? writing to me "you often say the beauty of poetry is that it is for the reader to interpret, and this is swirling around my brain like a coded message that I need to decipher – weird as it may sound!". I am from a family of 5, and my husband has always said, my story is the Cinderella story.

Well, if the shoe fits!!!

And The Clock Struck 12

The scullery maid runs ragged, in the rags she wears.
She dusts, she cooks, she cleans,
And the fabric tears,
a little more each day
Stepmother, stepsisters, are the hurdles she climbs
As she crawls in spaces of compassion left behind, a little sadder each day.
Fantasies colour her dreams, ribboned satin gowns.
Slippers of golden hue, sit perfectly on the ground, shinier every day.
On magical horses she rides,
To the ball where wishes can and do come true.
Miracles in abundance
She embraces her Xanadu, without delay
In the arms of ecstasy, dancing though the night
A prince in many colours,
Her heartbeat, pure delight, allowing her to play
Time was drawing near,
This strangest, strangers love
The ending become quite clear,
I must get out of here, and the clock struck 12!!
The gown disappeared,
Horses collapsed
Finery faded quickly
To a chorus of 'taps', and the clock struck 12.
She had reached the top,
Touching the rainbow
Orbiting the globe
Orphans dare not venture, now that dream was over.
Awaking with a start,
Ice in her veins
A stone in her heart,
Her soul in disgrace, for the rules, ignored.
Second hand dress
Second hand shoes
Her hair tied back
Time to sing the blues
And the clock stuck 12

Written again around midnight...I guess that's when the day's events are finally clear and have left the building.

My friend/fan wrote: "This one has some mind blowing verses and feels 'complicated' and I truly love it for its complexity."

I make her 100% correct. It is complicated... just rereading it now while assembling this text for my poetry book, Volume 2... and finding my favourite stanza... (pause while I consider)...
and the winner is......

"as you tackle the ugly, and redefine the signs, you shackle the hungry and rewrite the lines..."

Lest we forget, I am a true Gemini... and we are like onions... layer after layer after layer... and... we can make you cry... and... you can make 'us' cry... easily, I might add.

The flip side is, we can also make you laugh till your sides ache.

Moments

To live in this moment, what does this mean?
To ignore past mistakes, and pretend to be clean?
To whitewash your sins, as ignorance prevails.
But, guilt burns within, and regret blows your sails.

To live in the moment, is not easy to do.
Escape in the fast lane, that's how you get through.
As you tackle the ugly, and redefine the signs,
You feed the hungry, then rewrite the lines.

To live in the moment, is to defy destiny
But karma's a bitch, the witness to fallacy.
Ghosts of yesterday, disturb your nights peace,
As you watch your strategy, unfold, and release.

And you lie in bed, alone, but not lonely.
The movie rolls past, filled with 'if only's.
To be in the moment, is it possible to do?
When a lifetime of memories, scream out at you.

In the moment, in this moment I shall stay.
Yet the future shouts to me, and my past wants to play.
I cry for the innocence, sweet child of youth.
I embrace my heartbreak; her name is truth.

Moments of smiles, moments of sadness
Flashes of perfection, things you can't forget
You see the big picture, you pick and you choose
Hey, take your moment… you ain't got nothing to lose

Nothing but another 'moment'.

Whoops... there it goes!

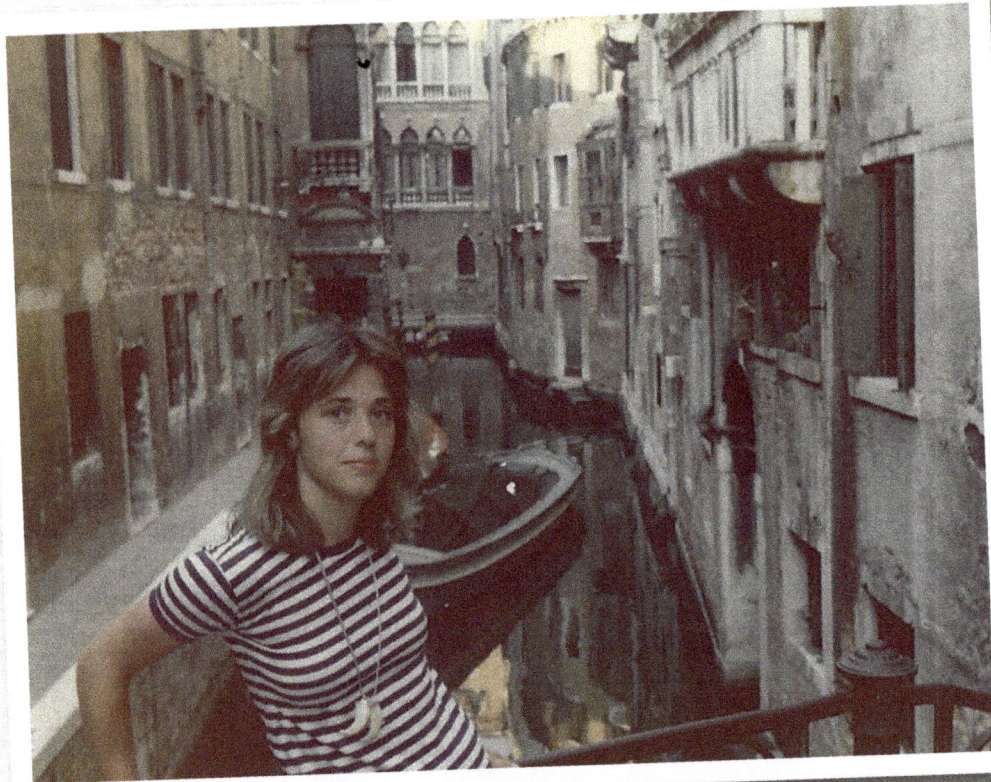

• *Venice, unfathomable, unattainable, unbelievable, and so loveable.*

This next poem is reflecting on my life... something you tend to do for various reasons.

And I will list them.

1. Questioning your judgement,

2. Hurting about an injustice,

3. Causing an injustice,

3. Feeling guilty,

4. Feeling lonely,

5. Feeling childish,

6. feeling old... or... all of the above.

This is the prelude, now here's the poem...

Dive in, but be careful you don't drown...... it's deep!!!

Hindsight

'Tis a wonderful thing,
If only we knew that,
In hindsight.

Exaggerated behaviour,
Exonerate the rest,
Until it all comes out in your favour.

Do you know that feeling? Sure, you do.
When your eyes begin to open,
And clear thoughts can pass through.

And your mind begins to flower
With such sweet perfume,
Deep feelings to savour,

Hindsight,
when the ghosts of mistakes
Haunt your desires.

"I did my best",
Sings the choir.
Shame's quagmire.

Hindsight
Morality speaks, midnight whispers
Demanding perfection,

But it's just a slide and a slipper,
Weaving a tale of woe
Hey, you were always a big tipper.

Hindsight,
Wrap me in your charms,
Protect me from rejection

The mirror of my life shines bright
My failures are my expectations,
The sword has been sharpened.

As our battle begins,
I bow to confrontation.
And accept the situation.

Hindsight,
Emotions in flow
You cannot stop this show.

Demons and dragons
Call you insane
Nothing to lose, everything to gain.

The pen is mighty
The ink dries clear
Truth, has nothing to fear

Hindsight,
Heaven or hell
Will my faith treat me lightly?

The soul is strong
I state my case
Will the death of 'us', delight me?

Hindsight,
Dark on the edge of light,
Alone, in the dead of night.

Can 'your' God digest this
Will you stay where you fall
Will you care at all?

Hindsight,
It's a wonderful thing
But oh, what a sting.

The thrust behind this poem is that no matter who you are, rich, poor, famous, unknown, female, male, said in the most gender friendly way... that no one matter what you do... how you write it, how you live it, what you make of it, wherever your road may take you... life is a series of patterns.. and they will weave their way, with or without you...because we are all wired how we're wired, and although we may blow a fuse sometimes....we are STILL wired the way we're wired... and my friend/fan's comments were ...

Lots of intriguing lines that beg for questions, but the ones that struck me particularly are..."but there's no happy ending, without some bending, a job that's always mine"... and adds....why is the job of bending always yours?... .because...

WE ARE WIRED
THE WAY WE'RE WIRED!!!

Questions anyone?

Patterns

Patterns of life,
Pete and re-peat.
From the top on my busy brain
To the bottom of my insecurity
I go cold, and retreat.

Falling into the illusion,
Of once upon a time,
But there's no happy ending,
Without some bending
A job that's always mine!!

Delving down to my needs
If only, if only, if only.
There's only one question,
And only one answer
God bless the lost and lonely

Patterns of life
Finding strength in weakness
No pretence, no façade
No masquerade, no mystery
Just the hurt I wear, defenceless

Patterns of life, Pete and re-peat
Trap me in contempt
With familiar waves of content
And this pattern is complete
Yes the pattern is fait'acompli.

• *My Amy and me in Mallorca....so happy.*

And another midnight offering...

In our apartment, Mallorca, not ready to sleep, so rummaging through the drawers, seeing what's in there... and to those who cannot guess who this is about... for once I will name the person, whose picture is above... its my granddaughter Amy, who has often shared this bed with me on numerous trips, now studying philosophy at Reading University.

Applause, love and gratitude for choosing me as your grandmother.

TO US!

On the right side of the bed,
I rummage through the drawer
Full of child's games and things,
Now, a child no more.

3 framed pictures,
A jewellery box below,
Notes inside a paper notebook
Saying, "I love you Joe"

All mixed up together,
Toys and grown-up ways,
I will always remember
That child, my heart, those days.

Snapshots of 'happy'
Flicker through my mind
I will hold on to these pictures,
Of all we've left behind.

As we step into tomorrow,
With no ado or fuss.
Our love remains alive
 I raise my glass to 'us'.

This next poem happened over a dinner in Hamburg.

It was a very pleasant evening and the conversation covered every topic under the sun. A phrase was said to me during the course of the evening, which my soul had an immediate reaction to... I even wrote it down on a scrap piece of paper, in between sipping my champagne, and trying to get back to concentrating on the conversation.

When I got home, that very evening, I adapted the phrase into how I had heard and interpreted it. One of those poems that just came flying out with no help from me... if that makes sense!! God how I love these kinds of evenings. They don't happen all the time. I am a communicator, and what follows is the result of true communication happening...

a moment caught in time!!

Don't Forget To Remember

Autumn leaves of red and gold, blow across a faded green lawn.
One season ends, another begins, we greet this brand new dawn.

And your thoughts turn to treasured memories, bicycle rides and childish pursuits.
Splashing around in shallow puddles, in knee high waterproof boots.

Storing photos in your mind, as cold air creeps in.
You leave this fall behind, nature rules, captures and wins.

Your thoughts turn to snowflakes of wonder, how beautiful the hanging icicles,
Skating on frozen ponds, adoring winter's spectacles.

Then, without warning, your woollen sweater's too warm.
You cautiously surrender, to this brand new season, with a different storm.

Spring creeps in slowly, with its rain, its thunder, its lightening.
Yet you awake with lightness of step, this new beginning to your liking!

Thoughts of adolescent dreams, when you wished upon a star.
With the road stretched out before you, a map to who you now are.

Mr. Sun rises with a vengeance, bringing days of summers scent.
And, those days of lazy and hazy, are proof of time well spent.

Now autumn has returned, it's the autumn of *your* years,
Whose leaves have all but fallen on a few unshed tears.

Don't deny history, your fire, your flaming embers,
Your world was as you made it, so don't forget to remember.

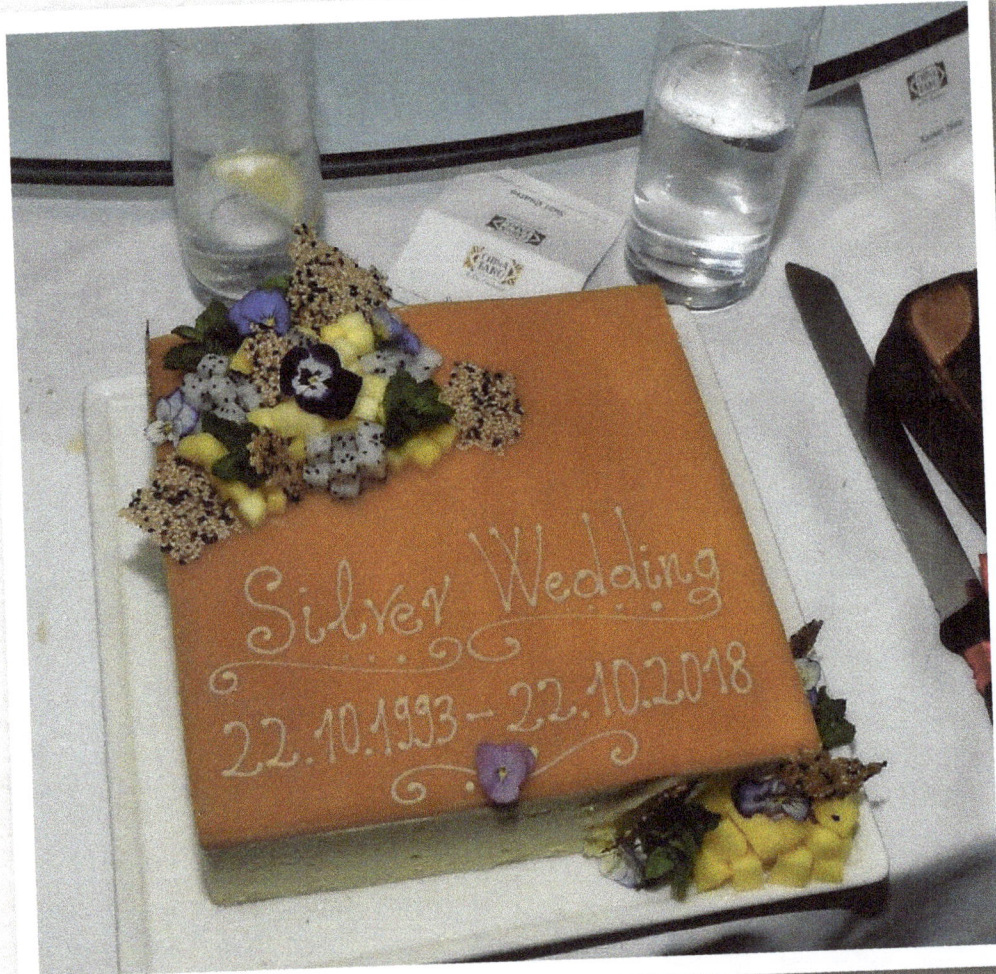

• *Big party in London... 'we did it... we are STILL doing it"*

One of 'those' poems.. where the less said, the better...
a little angry, a little disillusioned,

Just.. a little........(put in an adjective of your own choice)

Battles Of The Wills

Trust, honour, respect
3 words, 3 simple words.
Aim, fire, eject,
A shot, no one heard,
In this battle of the wills.

Take it all, it's yours,
With restrictions of course.
My watchdog shall guard you,
A measure of my force,
In this battle of the wills.

Not my children, on no.
No need to provide.
Yet the past reaches out,
With feelings, I cannot hide,
In this battle of the wills.

No watch dog for her, oh no,
No need to sanctify.
For she is the pedestal,
On which my needs rely,
In this battle of the wills.

Double the time, can't beat this crime,
Of no marriage, and no result.
No children, for the future,
No salvation, no default,
In this battle of the wills

And for loves' next contender,
This innocent bystander,
Ready to sling her hook
In her heart, within its candour
In these battles of the wills

YOU WIN!!!

This is one of the poems born out of the complete frustration of Lockdown...

you begin to wonder who you are, you question every relationship, even the one with yourself, you don't recognise the person looking back at you in the mirror, you exist on Skype, trying to make it count for something... life is just plain HARD...

But... it must be said... at least it is a life... so forgive me my bad temper... better out than in.

The Wake-Up Call

Months of being apart,
Circumstance beyond control.
Painting an alternate picture
Of a world we used to know.
Making do with communication
Victims of internet's console.
Accepting this situation,
No choice, for we have NO control.

Do we still belong together?
Was it only one moment in time?
And, if it's not forever,
Does our love, define the crime?
I set my alarm tonight,
One hour before I am needed.
Is this what it's all about?
Routine is so deep seeded.

It's Cinderella's ball,
Pumpkins, horses and a gown,
A fairy tale, a happy ending
As fantasy surrounds.
And when that fantasy fails
And the reaper rings his bell,
You face your grim reality
And accept it, heaven or hell.

As I fall into my slumber
A little worse for wear
A trip, a stumble, a blunder,
And perhaps… a little prayer

RING RING… omg.

THE WAKE-UP CALL
… better get outta bed.

• *Rainer and me on right, Me on left, and us getting married bottom left.*

This next poem went through a re-write as sometimes happens.

While assembling the book, finding the right order, re- reading everything... I actually wrote on this one a big ???'needs work'...

and it did... it has now become one of my favourites.

The title does pose a question... do we have a 'soul mate'... mmmmm and is there only 1 per lifetime?... mmmmmm... read on.

Soul Mate

Soul mate,
It's a strange concept.
Our first L-word
Our first F- word,
Soul mate, or Lust mate,
Mind and body, intercept.

Sleepless nights,
Counting lovers, not sheep.
The baaaaad 's and the gooooods'
Ten, twenty or more,
Surely not that many?
Were you really that naughty?

Soul mate,
Which one of them
Has stood the test of time
Which of them can still,
Transmit that secret sign.
Were any of them worth a dime?

Every love affair, even the one-night
stands
Was there a reason?
Did they make you happy?
Did they make you believe?
Or, did they make you grieve,
A soul mate for every season.

Now your autumn is upon you,
And your leaves are turning brown,
Why not leave the window open?
Till the snow hits the ground,
Sweet dreams to keep your hopes in
Till icebergs surround.

Soul mate,
And you simply obsess
Did you ever even know them?
Did your fantasies undress,
Did your failings swallow them?
Exposing your distress?

Soul mate,
If you really exist
Come and rescue me
With a scorching kiss
And I will thank thee
With my mask of bliss.

This armour you wear,
Is rusted and worn,
The beating in your chest
Weary and torn,
Tall on loves' battlefield,
Hoping to be reborn.

Soul mate,
If 'we' cannot come true
We must find a compromise
Between us two.
My soul mate, if love is blind,
Can we somehow, intertwine?

Because……

I will love you… my soul mate…
Till the end of 'our' time.
You 'are' my soul mate,
You complete my design.

There were many moments like the one that prompted this next poem.

Being locked down, being alone, watching endless programs on TV that you honestly have no interest in, just taking up time, and thinking thinking thinking... going down that woe is me path contemplating your navel, just 'down there'... you know what I mean.

A necessary journey to get to a better day in your soul... and... what's even more confusing is I am a 'glass half full' girl... and if the truth be known, between 2020 and 2022, my glass was a little too often, half full... wink wink.

It's Time

PRELUDE, sitting here alone, candle lit, film finished.
I am silent, I am thinking, I am feeling.
Damn it, I have something to say,
And I'm going to say it.
IT'S TIME, to cut out the dead weight
Throw out the flotsam,
Jettison the trash,
Rejoice, and then some.

IT'S TIME, to free my heart,
To kill the guilt,
Rip the rules apart,
Enjoy what I've built.
IT'S TIME, to leave dead relationships,
Family, friend or foe,
All those hardships,
Not needed anymore.

IT'S TIME, to reap what I've sowed,
Despite the pain
To retain what I'm owed
No loss, no gain!
IT'S TIME, to be in harmony
With all I am
The choices I have made
This person, since 'I' began.

IT'S TIME, IT'S TIME, IT'S TIME,
And I will take my time
With all my strength and power,
Before 'my' time is over.
IT'S TIME, to blow out the candle
Climb the stairs
Live the dream
Because I dare to dare!

IT'S TIME, tick... tock... tick... tock... tick... tock...
BONG!... (time's up)

• *First band, 1964, first band photo, and I guess this was the first day of the rest of my life.*

Sitting alone on tour for the second time in Australia in 2019, in my hotel room, hubby didn't come on this one, just too much traveling said he... and maybe he was right.
Anyway, left me lots of time to compose.

The subject email to myself says:
lyrics, ideas from Australia, 12:30 a.m.

But, as happens sometimes... this is better as a short and simple verse, so... here it is

Another Level

All goodbyes are kinda sad,
But this one goes deep.
All the heartbreaks I've had,
This pain, is pain I must keep.

Don't call me till you need me,
That's what is said.
Transatlantic communication,
And then, the line went dead!

The start and the finish,
And all that's in between,
Our script has been written,
And now... this final scene?

Another level to climb,
Another level to survive,
These strong arms tactics,
Keep 'this' love alive.

And on and on we go……

A verse written during the covid years, wow, I just wrote this as if the covid years are over,

When in fact... we have to live with the virus.
I was immersed in a blue funk, going day to day, wondering what was the point of waking up...

I explored these feelings in depth in my 'through my thoughts' musings, inspired by my daily instagrams ... reading this one, it's the same page, same thought, same emotion, same omg... when will this ever stop.

The Night Is My Enemy

First subconscious thought before I awake,
Am I alive or dead?
You would have thought it was obvious, wouldn't you?
Not the start of a new day, but a continuation of the same day,
Sigh……sigh….sigh.

Open the house,
Off with the night lights
Good coffee and bad news,
No end in sight
Oh my... oh my... oh my.

Morning passes without a sound,
Afternoon fades to evening,
Which is when I hit the ground.
Not the end of a new day, but the end of the same day.
Why... why... why...

The night is my enemy,
And I treat it with respect.
It's armed and it's dangerous,
Yet I know what to expect.
Cry... Cry... Cry.

I bow to the universe,
Of which I have no control,
The night is my enemy
And will witness tears as they flow.
Die... die... die.

Sigh... Oh my... why... cry... die.
The night is my enemy.

- *Portrait Dexter Brown, Bass and guitar, same family, Mr. and Mrs. Fender*

This originally was a song... and, there is a demo of it...
but it is a song that will never be sung again.

I wrote it during my lost year of being single for the first
time after 20 years together... confused, sad, lonely, and just
a little crazy...

I hope these adjectives are past tense!!!
She said tongue firmly in cheek.

Tumblin' Down

I don't want to fall,
don't want to give it all away
So don't make me cry,
Don't make me sad to say goodbye
Everybody bleeds,
Everybody needs a little pain,
So don't make me die,
Don't make me sad to say goodbye.

Come on the walls are tumblin' down,
come on the walls are tumblin' down
Come on the walls are tumblin' down,
come on the walls are tumblin' down

Then the walls, came tumblin' down
Yes the walls, they came tumblin' down
All I seek in my heart, can be found
Cuz you make my walls, come tumblin'down.

I don't want to feel,
don't want these feelings to be real
How I need you so,
Don't make me scared
To let you go

And, if my fear will subside,
Can you heal the child inside.

Come on the walls are tumblin' down,
come on the walls are tumblin' down
Come on the walls are tumblin' down,
come on the walls are tumblin' down

I'm scared.

I went back and forth with this one, because I love it so much... I wanted to either start this poetry book with it, or end with it... but as I began to assemble, it fell into this place all by itself.

I remember composing this, sitting on my bed in Mallorca, Sept 22nd, 8:57 p.m... so not the usual time.

I actually read this one to my husband when I was done because I wanted his reaction. I was not disappointed. Even though English is not his first language.. (not mine either actually being American!!)... he completely got it. His comment when I had finished reading it was:

"You're still that little girl"!
Do you think that's why we're together?

There Was A Little Girl

There was a little girl, often under attack,
And therefore, under cover,
Most of the time, just to survive.
Chequered blue blanket, up to her chin,
Safe from the cold breeze, blowing in.

She never knew she was cute, she never cared,
Because, cute, was not what was important.
She did know she was special and had 'something'.
A 'something' that would get her through.
Charm wrapped 'round... negativity did surround.

Tripping over cracks and scars, her heart, her soul.
On her mental express train she travelled.
Getting on board... go go go!
Flinging against the wall, praying silently
Oh god oh god oh god, somebody see ME, please!!!

There was a little girl, who walked her own road,
Who fought her own fight and won, truth be told?
She paid the price of guilt and jealousy,
But she found her light
Within the controversy.

There was a little girl, gave the game a whirl,
Rode that rainbow, then made a little twirl.
Belly full of fire, dreams and desires
Blanket toe to chin
To protect that gift within

There was a little girl
She is still that little girl.

• 78/79 pink BC Riches all round... are you ready?.. let's rock n roll!

Will never forget this feeling... on my way to an actual gig that happened to slip through the virus's hold on the world, in Denmark... could not believe we were going... actually going to a show. Very strange... only one half of audience allowed in, and all seated with masks on.

"Hey do you all wanna go down to Devil Gate Drive"... MMMMMPPPPPHHHHHPHHHHH.

That's what is sounded like.

My friend/fan commented: "Love it how you ended with those iconic words from The Wild One... think this will be a favourite with your fan base"... and over to you, the reader.

Destination Normal

Crack of dawn plane ride,
soaring through the clouds,
Breaking through to clear skies
Gin and tonic and crosswords
Destination... NORMAL
Passport and vaccination proof.
Remove sunglasses to reveal tired eyes.
Waiting to be allowed,
Waiting to be stamped,
Destination... NORMAL
Grey metallic luggage belt lay silent,
Oh the anticipation for the start up,
Ding dong…here it goes!!!
Nervous, as each 'not mine' bag drops
Destination… NORMAL
One more check of vaccination proof,
Cautiously rolling bag, disbelief,
The doors open wide.
OH MY GOD... I'M HERE, I'M HERE.
Destination... NORMAL
Anticipation running high,
Studying lyrics on laptop.
New songs, new memories, new moves
Been so long… too damn long.
Destination... NORMAL
Do the vocal warm up
Study set list on the table
Make up laid out, comb, towel on chair,
Fisherman's, those friends of mine, lying there.
Destination... NORMAL
Change into the outfit
Boots, belt, choker and jacket
Start the backstage pacing
Stride to the side, bass on, ready
Arrival... NORMAL

"All my life I wanted to be somebody,
and here I am!"

Been in this house since 1980... the longest I have ever lived anywhere.

Next door I was lucky to have extremely nice neighbours. They watched my kids sometimes, they watched my grandchildren sometimes, they came to our house parties, they knew both sets of parents, my ex, and my husband of nearly 30 years now.
We were like family.

Once her husband, Patrick, had passed on, June (who shares my birthday!!), stayed there, surrounded by the house she loves filled with her memories, filled with her life. She has finally gone elsewhere to live to be looked after properly. Every single day when I wake up, I look out the window at the empty cottage and say out loud, "she's never coming back"... and she's not.

It makes me sad.

The Window

Grey and drizzle abound,
Trees sway in the breeze.
Mother nature whispers,
You're invited to my party,
No r.s.v.p, just come as you are, please.

Someone else's life stares back at me,
Uncompromising, unforgiving,
Her curtains have fallen,
Resting on the windowsill
Empty, empty... so empty and still

Walls soak up our energy
In this film with no preview,
Leaving residue of emotions
Swirling round and round,
Even when your six feet underground.

Looking at her window,
Many memories flash by
Running round my heart my mind,
Many years that have gone too fast
My window, her window, trapped in time.

Through her window, all is revealed,
Through my window, my vision clear
I gaze upon her loneliness
And hold this feeling dear.
There is nothing more to fear.

• *Vegas trip, thanks to dad, just before relocating in 1971..*
sometimes you just gotta gamble.

Looked at this poem several times... wondering where to place it...
thought it should be either first of last in the book... but the book has
moved on, as I have... and so... it's placed here.

I wrote the following concerning this poem...
Every relationship, every outcome, Every struggle, even with
yourself... which led me to composing this verse.

Needless to say, in 2019 with the release of Suzi Q, lots of emotions
were flying around from every corner and it was hard to come to
terms with it all.

Anyway, that was my mindset... and here is the poem.

Victory

Why am I so afraid to let this go?
Am I afraid I will lose something of myself if I do?
That's crazy, because the part I 'would' lose,
Would not be me, just the confusion.
It would be fear, that is 'was' a part of me
That would give me cause for concern.
And I would miss, and I would mourn,
I would yearn for this all to stop.
Never quite understanding the need
Never quite understanding the futility,
Only understanding the truth within my soul,
That I am, and always will be,
Dictated to by my emotions.
That I will always take the higher ground,
No matter how humiliating it may seem
Weakness say you... Strength say I.
Much easier to just walk away. Much!
For then you have nothing at all to face,
But your 'own' illusions,
Illusions with no conclusion
How sad is that!
I choose to stay... I choose to fight
I choose to pray... I choose the light
And always will.

To love is not to like
To accept is not to forgive
To hurt is not to feel...
But to be all you can be... that... is...
VICTORY.

This is one of 'those' poems.
These words were intended for a song,

A song that never came to fruition.
It hung around, taking up space in my lyric book
until I finally realised, it's for my next poetry book.

Re the title... everything, and I mean everything
interesting happens,

Between the beat!! So, pay attention.

Between The Beat

Between the beat, between the beat
I want to die, inside your heat.
Those things you hide, each time we meet.
Between our heat, between our beat.

Take a chance on this craziness
Devilish things you do,
Sweet child of lust I'm drawn
Into the sensualness of you.

I can dance upon the ceiling
Make your movie turn blue,
And this game you play so easily
It's a tango called taboo.

Been lost inside the wilderness,
love's consuming fire
Sweet angel of darkness, on the edge of desire.
I'll crawl in your sheets, give all you require,
Chained to the bedpost, let's fly that high wire

Between the beat, between the beat
I want to die... inside your heat.

• *Rainer and me and best man at wedding, and best friend since 1986...awww*

Have you ever met a married couple, or even just a dating couple, who say "We never argue"... well... first of all, I don't believe it... and second of all , If its true... all that means to me is they don't care enough!!! cynical or just realistic.

Who am I to judge anyway...

Just my humble.

Who Would Have Thought It?

Who ever thought I would meet,
Somebody like you?
Did you ever think you would meet?
Somebody like me?
I don't think so.
A person who challenges at every corner,
A person who pokes fun, at every opportunity.
And, getting personal now,
A person who rips up a drawing of my love for him,
Making me cry harder that I have ever cried.
But also,
A person who loves me for who I am,
A person who I love exactly as he is.
You have your demons, I have mine,
On this we can agree.
Your rough edges, mine, maybe rougher.
But still, our worlds do rhyme.

We belong together,
Even though we've fought it,
yes indeed, we belong together,
who would have thought it?

This was written at a gig, and it is dated
Oct 17th, 2013.

I remember sitting at a café, and having to
ask the waiter if he had a piece of paper and
a pen.

As I poured my latte down my throat,
this poured out of me.

On The Road

Here I sit, in a town square.
Czech people,
Chequered past,
Leading their checkered lives.

Market stalls
Fruit, and vegetables,
Bags, scarves and shoes,
"what do you need?"

What's your dream?
A bargain at half the price
I, the privileged observer,
Another gig, another town, another life.

- Look carefully folks, It's my dog, having his way with a stray cat who wanted feeding, awwww the price of a free meal eh!

My life, I guess like everyone in this world, has had its share of sorrow. Things happen, decisions are made, and, no matter how much you try and change it… it just won't, just can't, whatever the reason… it is what it is. I was obviously alone on this birthday so wallowing in the sadness of my situation, big time.

And, on the flip side… years later, I realize that the decision that was made was the correct one after all… WOW… all that, crying, arguing, screaming, scheming… all that GODDAMN PAIN for nothing. Lesson learned.

Reality is not always easy to reach, and once you have arrived, it's not easy to live there.

Realities

It's my birthday
Tears on my pillow,
You would have thought,
this would be a happy day,
would you not?
In reality... it's not.

Things are not right
Since the incident.
An incident I so wished
I had kept to myself.
I will never desert my heart,
In reality... no choice.

I wish I was someplace else,
In another world,
Suspended in space
Another time, another place
Where nothing hurts,
In reality... this does not exist

Happy birthday Gemini, God bless me
Good night or good morning,
Morpheus, be the man,
And sprinkle sand in my eyes
In reality... we sleep to escape.

Pleasant dreams because
Realities... are never sweet.

Writing this next one, really took it out of me. I had to dig so deep... you know what I mean, deep where the pain lives... rent free!

Interesting conversation with my friend/fan on this one, so I will quote her..."

Dooooooh, this is going to open the biggest can of worms ever once you release it. My favourite verse is "could it be that you dive down simply to be able to resurface? Must we all swim against the tide to prove our worthiness?"

And my favourite line is "are the scales of life responsible for balancing our emotions?"

And your favourite is???????????

Read on.

Too Much Sadness

Watching a midnight movie,
Buying into the plot.
Believing in the characters,
Relating it to real life?... as 'we' live it?
Or, as it lives us?
And of course, crying our eyes out.
When poignant moments, flash across the screen
Violins swelling in the background, so serene.
Question...
Why is there so much sadness?
Why is there so little happiness?
Is this a true statement?
Or, is it, in the words of Isaac newton,
"no action without re-action"?
Could it be that simple?
Are the scales of life responsible
For balancing our emotions?
Or... Entertain this thought...
Could it be that we enjoy our despair?
The futility, the 'woe is me',
Nobody understands me, when will I be loved?
This diving down into your pain, drowning in your tears,
Why me, oh my god, oh my god, why me??
Does nobody understand me, you ask again,
Expecting no reply.
STOP RIGHT THERE... JUST STOP.
Do 'you' understand you?
Could it be that 'you' are responsible?
For balancing your own emotions?
Could it be that you dive down,
Simply to be able to resurface?
Must we all swim against the tide,
To prove our worthiness?
Throw me a life jacket, while I ponder this.
Hopefully I will figure it out
before I go down for the 3rd time.

• "so.. what is love anyway?"

I was in a philosophical mood when I penned this next offering.

I was questioning what love actually is... plain and simple...
let the words speak for themselves.

Power You

When you love somebody
You give them POWER to hurt you.

When you truly love yourself,
This POWER belongs to you alone.

Do not collapse into a relationship
Do not expect anyone to make 'you' whole.

You are whole.

Remember that.

You, are a complete person,
You, are all you need
With your foibles, your quirks, your habits,

The good, the bad, and of course the ugly,
All have an equal share within
It's called being 'human'.

We are all born alone, our journey is ours alone,
We have a built-in compass, and a road map
With a few stops in between
Make sure your gas tank is full

We're born alone, and we die alone
Make your journey count.

POWER YOU, POWER YOU, POWER YOU.

This was one of those times when I was conversing with somebody, both on the phone and Email. Someone whose life had taken a big turn, and was pointing him in a completely different direction.

We shared stories and talked about emotional problems we had both been through.
And in fact, we talked very easily from the moment we met. I would say, kindred souls, with a helluva lot in common.

We were going to try and meet up for a drink before he left these shores but it didn't happen.
The line was said, 'Time has beaten us"...

And me being me...
I turned it into the following:

Time Has Beaten Us

Memories are funny things,
They creep upon us, on an empty street,
Ready to steal our valuables,
Making us feel vulnerable,
Then they turn, and quickly retreat.

Cloak and dagger, stealing our thoughts,
Reminding us of what we once had,
And have no more.
Love love love... da da da da da.
Is that all there is?
Feelings back on the shelf they came from.

A whispering wind, a caressing thought,
That sneaks into your mind, unexpected.
You can smell, you can taste, you can touch,
Familiarity in senses never to be lost.
Those knights in shining armour, ride off, into the night
Back to that dream they came from.

Memories are funny things,
They haunt us and comfort us, in the twilight hours.
Promising paradise, delivering hell.
I see cupid smiling… keep score.
The journey of the heart is perilous,
And I fear, my love… time… has beaten us.

• *Detroit, 60th birthday party, my suite!!!! fabulous*

And it must be said, since the majority of these poems have been written during the pandemic, and what followed in 2022, they do reflect all the confusion and loneliness we were all going through.

Also, the ongoing emotional difficulties with some family members.

That's always the hardest part to accept because of the L word and the M word getting in the way of objectivity... it's the way nature intended it.
(in case your wondering, L for Love.. and M for Mother).

Dark Tunnels

Sometimes I want to say goodbye,
To all the hardships of,
trying…To live in this world.
A world that doesn't accept individuality,
A world that doesn't promote sincerity,
A world that applauds mediocrity.

My energy, my light
My needs, my desires
My vision, my morals,
Caught in life's crossfire.

Compromise is a truce found,
Surrender is buried in the ground

Whoever I am, whatever I do
Let it be me, let it be mine
Let me 'shine' long after I am gone
May my memory linger on.

This can all be precious
Or mental flagellation
So many inadequate choices
Yet, self belief, needs no validation.

My perception, my truth
My questions, my answers
My acceptance, my peace
I'm one of life's dancers.

Dark tunnels
Dark days
I pray I can find my way.

*This one reflects my inner turmoil, probably
arguing about something with a loved one,
god knows what it was about... I surely can't
remember... the time it was written says it all.*

*In the twilight hours your brain does a twist,
you open your heart, you pick up you pen
and paper, or your laptop, whatever is handy
in the twilight hours, and you begin...*

and keep going until its over.

Random Thoughts, 4.15a.m.

Nothing to look at, nothing to do
An airless room, half light breaks through
How many minutes, how much time?
To do what I must do,
To own what is mine?

If the best is over, if the end is nigh
I wish you God speed,
I wish you wings to fly.
If the best is over,
If the end is nigh.

Nothing lasts forever
But hope dies last,
I thought I'd leave you 'never',
Not that dream is dying fast,
But hope dies last.

Is it all over now,
Is it the end?... HOW???

Random thoughts, 4:15 a.m.
Sunrise arrives, another day begins.

• Parents' 50th anniversary, sisters performed, the Golden Years, (S. Quatro), Patti, Arlene, mom, Sherry, dad, me and Nancy. Texas.

Sometimes one of your parents says something to you, that not only confuses you but stays with you for your entire life. This is one of the moments.

I am still confused by his words, and have still not been able to do as he requested. Sorry dad... up there 'singing with angels' for a long time now... but I just never did get this?

My fan/friend says, "this poem is dripping with vulnerability but also 'determination"... (spot on description of my character).

Toughen Up

A rough and tumble existence,
Was always the path of least resistance
How I stumbled, how I fell,
But my strength was my persistence.

So cold, there was no empathy,
Nor shelter, I found no sympathy.
So, I burned in the fires of disinterest,
But my strength was, I believed in ME!

A square peg in the roundest hole,
I was a lost and lonely soul,
How I struggled to survive,
This rock, that just had to roll.

"toughen up" my daddy said
Hide your weakness, fight instead!
So, I faced him, eye to eye
And killed his words, stone dead.

How can my heart pretend?
This softness, must I defend?
"Toughen up", What does this mean?
When the wounds, will always mend.

Do you question my integrity?
Did you doubt my sanity?
"Toughen up" has no meaning
But to cloud my humanity.

"Toughen up", has no sound
"Toughen up", can't be found
"Toughen up" my daddy said
Then his words, hit the ground.

And another one that sat around a long time in my lyric book...

And it belongs here. It is short and sweet and to the point. I had finished writing my autobiography which brought up a lot of issues and situations that had been buried a long time.

Keep your friends close, but your enemies closer.

Friendly No More

Friends aren't friends, when they're friendly no more

Friends aren't friends, when they'll kill you to score

All that turmoil inside, those secrets you both keep

All that sadness you cried, on the edge where orphans weep.

Till we're friendly no more.

Your harder than I ever pretended to be,

Harder than the bark, clinging to a tree

You set your sails in motion, and plotted your course,

Play havoc with my emotions, for I had lost my voice.

Friends aren't friends, when they're friendly no more

Friends aren't friends, when they'll kill you to score.

• *Xmas mid 90s, before I redecorated.. and a smiling hubby.. a result!!*

After writing that beautiful Xmas song with my son, released in 2021, My Heart and Soul (I need you home for Xmas)... and the uncertainty of would my husband actually be able to get to me... he literally caught the last plane out... with just a handful of passengers on board, and a nightmare getting through at Heathrow... but he made it.

This was written last Xmas, our first one we have ever spent alone due to all the restrictions coming in force, so, this time my husband 'didn't make it home for Xmas, and it wasn't easy.

Christmas Catch-22

It's okay, It's really okay.
Hope I have enough memories on tap
To make it to the end of this day.
White dust on the curtains,
Footsteps echo behind,
To this loneliness, I'm resigned,
But it's okay, it has to be okay.

Christmas lights twinkling
Nat King Cole crooning
"Silent night, holy night,"
fire steadily burning.
Ashes of my past,
Keys I am turning
Unwrapping, unlocking, at last.

Fifty years to the day
I walked London streets alone
Joining choirs of carol singers
A heart without a home.
Allowing memories to replay,
And, somehow, holding on.
Fifty years to the day.

White cloth on the table
Candle lit and warm
Empty chairs, empty places
I watch the movie unfold,
Haunting my thoughts,
Sad and distraught
Feeling a little unstable.

I wander room to room,
Arms outstretched to find,
Some happy, within the gloom
The meaning of the season sublime,
It's Christmas without me and you
It's Christmas the old and the new
It's Christmas... catch 22.

Yet another in in what seems to be one of my constant refrains. God only knows I must have really had a hard time in my childhood, remaining *WHO I AM*... and I think that struggle has continued to this present day.

It takes a lifetime of wins and loses, mistakes and successes, laughter, heartache, regrets, and everything in between to find out who you are, and then to stay true to who you are.

Still, mustn't complain. The fight has given me so much to write about... and here is another one.

To Be Honest

Yes, I am happy, but,
Within that 'happy'
Is a 'happy' that turns,
Into an upside-down smile.

To be honest

You can love but not like,
You can laugh, but not smile
You can hurt but not cry
You may not 'live', before you die!

To be honest.

The question is,
How do I feel?
I don't feel any 'more'
I don't' feel any 'less.'

To be honest.

I am not afraid,
Not like I used to be.
When I was wet behind the ears.
But I was the 'younger' me then,
I needed to learn to like 'me'.

To be honest.

I won't change who I am
I can't change who I am
And if I am alone,
That's okay

To be honest.

• Home Sweet Home.. mom on left, dad on right..so comforting.

Who can ever explain or even understand exactly what love is, yet it is the basis of so many songs, plays, movies... never ending.

The following take on it.
My fan/friend made this very short comment "awwwwwwwww, and that's all I am going to say about this poem"

Love Is...

Even when we're apart,
We are together
You live inside my heart,
And that beat will beat, forever.

Even when we disagree,
Both egos flying,
The truth is in the middle,
And we reach it, with neither of us dying.

Even when we shut down,
Stubborn and unyielding,
Riding waves of won't relent,
We can never deny this feeling.

Love is a warmth that glows
Love is the poet's delight
Even without light to grow,
Love will always shine bright

Love is......

I Remember where I was when this next offering appeared. I am pretty sure it followed quickly on the heels of 'Fame of Famine'. A little obscure, a little different, but interesting I would say.

I have a room I sit in at our Hamburg home, and I often sit there most of the day, either playing my bass, or working on poems, or playing my online word games. It's very quiet usually... lots of time to think.

My fan/friend commented:

"Wowza Suzi, where did that come from? This is good, This is VERY VERY good."

And I humbly take a bow.

Fractions

Fractions of nothingness, casting shadows,
A grey couch, a grey ceiling and a stained grey window.
A black widow.
A dead lover.
Hard to notice that silken thread,
Up and down, back and forth, tightly wound.
She skitters 'cross the floor,
Setting the trap, to which the key,
Remains unfound!

A fly buzzing crazily around,
desperate to escape.
Fractions of nothingness
Fractions of emptiness.

Once so alive,
Sky highing, sky diving, buzz buzzing,
CAUGHT!!
Now... dying.
In this tangled web she weaves.
Beating his wings weakly,
Slow and slower… until…
They beat no more.

Fractions of nothingness
Hazy shadows surround.
Fractions of nothingness
A scream, without a sound.

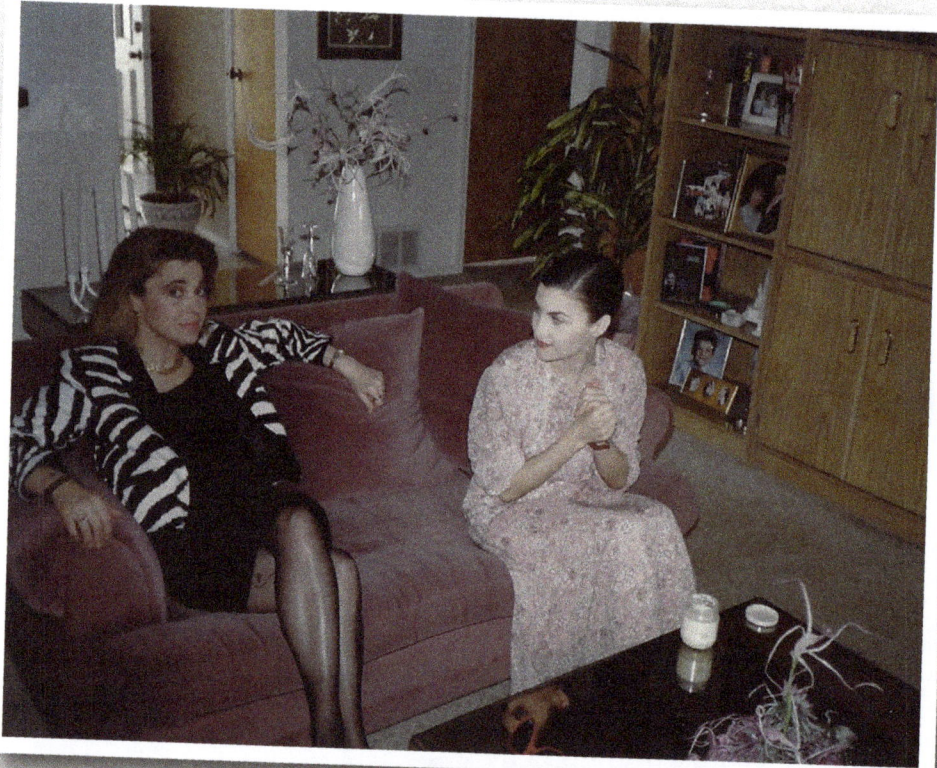

• 50th anniversary, me and niece Sherry.. Nancy's house.

I was born and raised a Catholic, and that stays with you a lifetime, and thank God it does. With all that has been happening in the world, it makes you consider many different things, judgement day being one of them.

This verse was written while I was pondering the absolute fact that one day, I will not be here. Funny enough it doesn't frighten me.... why should it... it's a foregone conclusion, that eventually comes to us all.

My fan/friend said "some seriously sombre musing at play in this poem, but most important, some undeniable truths."

Read on folks.

Judgement Day

It's that time in our lives for reflection,
Who, what, and why…are now paramount?
Although age may be a small factor,
There is no age that truly counts.

Reassessing and reapproaching,
Rebuilding bridges that have burned.
And the only thing that really matters,
Are the lessons we have learned.

Time is precious, life is short,
Too damn short, to sit in judgement.
We all deserve a voice in this world,
No matter how crude, or, eloquent.

When I lay upon that pillow,
My final destination.
I will not ask the reason,
Nor make any accusation.

Judgement day will arrive,
When you least expect it.
Judgement day will thrive,
We all must respect it.

And when the outcome is tallied,
Between wrong and right,
Which side will you sit upon,
Heaven or hell, dark or light?

Yes, judgement day will arrive,
So, you best, get your deeds in order.
Only judgement day will survive,
Us mortals, simply cross the border.

I remember very well writing this verse. It went through quite a few tweakings, because the subject matter is very dear to my heart, very important, and expresses and ongoing situation in my life.

This situation is fraught with landmines, wrong turns, precipices, storms, and many rivers to cross.

It's one of my longer verses, I would suggest you read this slowly and carefully.

Only A Bridge

There's this fractured relationship,
Broken in pieces.
A muddy slope on which we slide,
As the blood inside our veins, freezes.
But when you gaze into the face of it,
It's only a bridge, why can't I cross it?

This worn-out jagged anger
That just rolls on and on.
A red flag, that spells danger,
Zero tolerance precedes the dawn.
And when you gaze into the face of it,
It's only a bridge, why won't you cross it?

There's no need for blame or shame,
No reason to disentangle.
It's the mankind in all of us,
So… what did you bring to the table?
Yes, when you gaze into the face of it,
It's only a bridge, why won't 'we' cross it?

Our hearts, torn and rusted
With sadness and disrepair,
Our hopes, now done and dusted,
And it all seems so unfair!
And, as we gaze into the face of it,
It's only a bridge, will we ever cross it?

Standing on the precipice
Calm before the storm,
Staring into emptiness,
No heat to keep us warm.
Yet, as we gaze into the face of it,
It's only a bridge, do we dare cross it?

A white feather lands at my feet,
The message is quite clear.
There is nothing love cannot defeat,
So, I walk 'into' my fear.
I stare defiant in the face of it.
It's only a bridge. CAN we cross it?

And, I whisper softer to the retreating tide...
"take my hand... let's get to the other side.

It's only a bridge

WE CAN CROSS IT.

• *I am sailing on the sea of life, taking control, my map, my destiny.*

Sometimes you must look around at your life, at the space you occupy, at the possessions you have accumulated, where you place value, where you do not, you need to take stock every now and again, and that is what this next one is all about,

Me taking stock. My fan/friend asked the question, "this is a game of pros and cons about your life, is in not?

Guilty as charged.

Observations

The end of the evening is nigh,
Playing word games with my mind.
Pleasure, relaxation, with candle lit ambiance.
Staring at this movie of mine,
A preview that won't quit.
I observe, it's not over yet!

I wander through my memory,
My God, the road I've travelled.
Possessions, obsessions, as trappings unravel.
Gold records on the wall,
Success echoes round
I observe this empty hall.

Treasures we accumulate,
placing value on things.
Statues, paintings, nectar of the gods,
Just roundabouts and swings.
My successes, my misbehaviours
I observe my wins and failures.

A slice of heaven, these panelled rooms
Mother nature surrounds, I'm safe in her womb.
Sympathise, self-analyse, ego on the floor.
I crawl into solitude's space,
As fear rears its head.
I observe the life I've led.

Counting your blessings, is sometimes a curse
Hailing the best and defending the worst.
Interludes of platitudes, then applause dies away.
So many energies, have been here to play.
Proof of a past this mirror cannot hide,
I observe my reflection, with honesty and pride.

And 'that's an observation worth having.

I was flying to Hamburg, doing my usual crossword puzzles. Once again a piece of paper fell out of the book that I had obviously started and not finished on another previous airplane journey, since I always use the same crossword book when I travel.

Hey, I thought, this is good, and so I finished it... and suddenly, the flight was over.

Suddenly

8 miles high
On an evening flight.
Airport like a ghost town,
No life in sight.

Piccolo on the tray
2 games on the go.
Hurtling through the skies,
And knowing what I know.

Oh my god, he really loves me!
Is it more than I deserve?
This reality hits me,
Right down to the nerve.

Why didn't I realize,
All those years gone by.
My soulmate, my heart
Was there, right by my side.

Suddenly I knew,
No more wondering why
My search was finally over,
Suddenly I'm 'here'.

• circa 1974, choker and tiger's eye necklace.. still have choker... still fits!!

This next poem happens to everyone.

We love, we fall out of love, we love again, and fall out again...
without any rhyme or reason... and that is what I tried to do....
make sense out of it by writing about it.

Interesting exchange between my fan/friend and myself about this
poem, worth quoting... she wrote:
"It's another very good poem and for some reason, one that left me
a little unsettled."...

I replied, "Good, that was my intention, writing it left me unsettled
too... in fact, living it, leaves me unsettled.

Midnight Musings

Midnight musings speak to me,
I have no choice but to listen.
Daylight covers multitudes of sins,
Shielding doubts, that challenge vision.
Grow together or grow apart
Is there any other?
Maybe there's another chance,
Somewhere, hidden 'neath our cover.
It was all so much easier,
When attraction was glowing.
Arguments and opinions,
Just juices flowing.
Now it's down to blame,
Don't say this, don't look like that.
Then lashing of apologies,
But your excuses leave me flat.
I wonder what it's all about
The wheres, they whys, the whethers.
Why torture our souls,
Should we still be together?
Midnight musings call to me,
I have no choice but to listen
Out of tune, or harmony
Oh god, the indecision.
Sandman bring me a dream,
One I will recall.
Sprinkle stardust at my feet,
And cushion this final fall.
Every beginning has an end,
No matter how you try
Every smile has a tear,
Love is the reason we cry.

Midnight musings call me,
I have no choice but to listen
Please hold me in your arms,
And wrap me in your wisdom.

This was born out of the situation the world is going through politically, as I was writing this, hopefully it will be over by the time this book is out.

Very scary times, watching the news every day, almost afraid to watch the news, but it's kind of like a car accident... you must look!

For this one I created a poet, a gentle, peace-loving person observing the world, and trying to speak it pretty, but it was no use.

One of my favourites.

The Poet

You arrived the poet,
Wearing your words,
You left cold and naked,
Because nobody heard.

Power mad tyrants,
Indiscriminate fools,
Intent on destruction,
They ignore nature's rules

Danger is alive and kicking
It's a tense situation.
Just the push of one button,
Who cares, the condemnation.

No justice prevails,
This inhumane explosion
Each peaceful heart falls
Into their emotion.

You arrived the poet,
Wearing your words.
You left cold and naked,
Because nobody heard.

A....MEN.

• *Xmas - favourite of time of year, was always a happy time... mmmmmmmm*

Maybe it's an age thing, maybe it's going through the years of Covid, maybe it's just reflection and again taking stock of your life... and maybe it's simply... maybe and whatever may be.

My fan/friend said:
"don't know what mood you were in when you wrote it, but this made me feel sad"... Well... we all got to feel sad sometimes!!!

And remember, when your done feeling sad, the 'happy' comes in......maybe.

Sometimes

Sometimes,
My thoughts whirl around
Like a tornado.
A sneaky smile,
A quiet tear,
This movie with no sound.
My thoughts whirl around.

Sometimes I wonder,
As I lay upon my bed,
Feeling my turmoil
Flowing like lava,
Reliving ways I've bled.
As I lay upon my bed.

Sometimes
I can remember,
Every wayward step.
Good intentions can be lost
to moral surrender.
Yes, I can remember.

Sometimes
My thoughts whirl around
Like a tornado
The wins, I exaggerate
The tragedies, underground,
My thoughts whirl around

And another long one... and again about prevailing family issues, we all have them, nobody escapes, and I mean nobody.

I remember one time I was doing a Q & A after one of the premieres for my documentary, Suzi Q, which would have been 2019, early 2020 before the world changed.

Since it is my life story, of course some family related questions were asked, to which I tried to reply honestly and kindly.

No need for a long explanation of the thrust of my next offering, it's all there.

The Dilemma

If blood is thicker than water, a thin line between love and hate,
If one can't exist without the other, let's accept, it's not too late.
One daughter, one mother, a son, sister and brother,
Family ties knot and mangle, taking it out on one another.

Love is not the question, but like, that's another matter.
We are wrestling the toss, but, no winners to disable.
We've had our darkest moment, within our share of tears.
In depths of despair we've sunk and suffered many years.

Let's focus on the positive, laughter and smiles.
Let's find a reason to believe and sit with that awhile.
It doesn't really matter, angry words get thrown,
When all is said and done, sadness is ours alone.

When the reaper calls, I will follow where he leads.
And know this verse was written, by a pure heart, that bleeds.
Read this while I'm here, read this when I am gone.
Ashes to ashes, dust to dust, my words will linger on.

Family loves a true dilemma, land mines and barbed wire,
No escape from troubled water, we all sink in bloods' mire.
Family loves a true dilemma who the hell can understand.
Lay down your weapons and meet me,
I'm reaching out, just take my hand.

This dilemma, this dilemma, no blame, no shame, no guilt,
This dilemma, this dilemma, shake foundations of all we've built
As we end what has begun, these words will ring true.
No matter what was said and done, I will always love all of you.

- *50th birthday Berlin, 'if these are the cards I was dealt, happy to ante up and keep playing my hand.*

This seemed to cause a little confusion in my fan/friend, and she had more than a few questions... which I answered.

She questioned the 'happy' in the last stanza, to which I replied, I will stand by the last line 100%... it is the only way I have survived, because, I am true to myself... even if the price is high, meaning I get hurt a lot.... I am HAPPY with my sadness, hope this clarifies it... .and it did. Beautiful, emotional, and yes, .. a little tearful.

These are the cards I was dealt, and these are the card play. "know when to hold em, know when to fold em"... Roger that, (Kenny)

The Victim

So, if they pay the piper,
And they call the tune,
Will a hidden sniper
End this song too soon?

Who brandishes control,
In the rhythm of the night?
It lures you to the dance floor,
And traps you in the spotlight.

Your motivation may be pure,
But manipulation rules.
As you're caught unawares,
On this ship of fools.

Feel the softest touch
Of the gentlest hand,
It's a touch too much
And you sink in their quicksand.

If the victim writes the song,
If the victim calls the tune.
Will she be another casualty?
Will her song end too soon?

Dream a little dream with me,
A victim, I may always be.
But to myself I must be true,
And the song I sing, is... 'happy'.

This is one of those very descriptive poems - you can picture the scene, you can feel the space and air surrounding me, you see me gazing out the window, thoughts swirling round until they conclude and the pen goes to the paper.

Such a magical moment when it all comes together. I can never get enough.

My fan/friend wrote,
"Did reading Nietzsche, the 'king' of nihilism, set the mood for the poem? Reading through it, I'd say most definitely yes!.."

Well.. I must agree with you. He sure did put a different spin on my thoughts, or maybe he just clarified them for me.

Yesterday, Today, Tomorrow

Autumn sunlight through the glass
Sitting on the window seat.
A flute of champagne,
Billie Holiday on the stereo,
Nietzsche on my lap.

Questioning, that's all.
Just questioning.
Reading, digesting,
Wondering how I got here,
My mind in a flap.

It was all written
Before I was born,
I am merely the caretaker,
Of the secrets of time,
And the world will spin without me.

Yesterday is gone,
Today is but a glimpse,
Tomorrow is a hope
To conquer mortality,
I know, this world will spin without me.

- *Leather Forever Encore Tour, QSP opened up the show, Rainer's bday, Andy Scott, Rainer, Pat Doonan, Don Powell, me, Harley and Maria Medcalf*

I remember how this one happened.

I was sitting at my dining room table, flicking through my 'ideas' book - phrases, titles, one liners... and I found one particular page of random thoughts added at different times, which all fitted together like a tapestry. You could say, it wrote itself.

My fan/friend commented: "There are parts of this I can relate to, "don't lose your lonely, don't lose your soul, it's just love... in flow".

Enough said. Let the poem speak now.. SH!!!!! Read and Digest.

Odd Lines and Misdemeanors

Like a butterfly, I'm free, I'm free.
Is this something to do with me,
You cry?

I can intimidate at 10 paces,
I'm tough as nails,
I reply.

Our car has crashed, dream smashed,
So, who's gonna pay the bill?
Not I.

Negativity is poison, I won't drink alone,
Or this emotional orphan inside,
will die.

I won't lose lonely, I won't lose soul,
It's all just love in flow,
No need to ask why.

You'll never let me fall, Empty words, that's all
I fell fast and hard,
Down to earth from the sky.

Back to the room, back to the gloom
Back to that cracked mirror
To justify.

Grey day news, grey day skies
I've ridden the storm
From the lows to the high.

I will paint my dreams
of rainbows and sunbeams,
And I don't need wings to fly.

So, coming to the next offering.. which is extremely short... sometimes its like that isn't it... you can say everything you need to say in a few short sentences.

I am reading in my notes, dated oct 3, 2021, 09:24 a.m. "posted on Facebook and tweaked... and realized it would be nice in my next poetry book..

here it is.

Untitled

I HAVE DECIDED,

TAKING A BREAK FROM IT ALL

FOOT OFF THE GAS,

BODY, MIND AND SOUL.

NEED TO RELAX,

SO

WHERE'S ALL THIS WIND THEY KEEP TALKING ABOUT?

AIN'T NOTHING BLOWING OUT MY WINDOW.

JUST A COUPLE OF ANSWERS…. MAYBE!

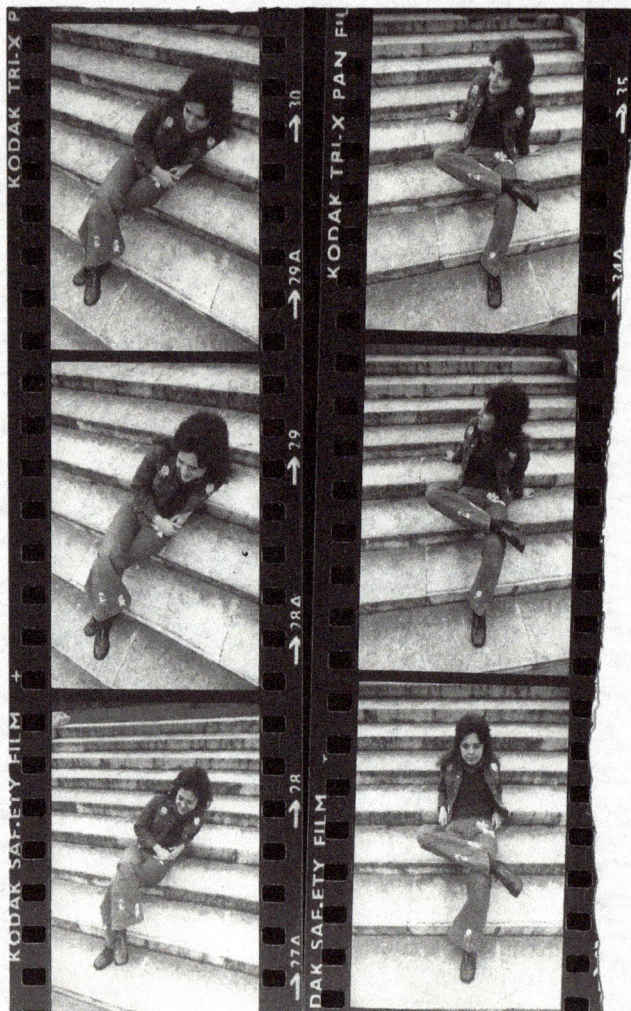

• *1972... sitting on the stairway to success...*
what a long hard climb it turned out to be

Next up... obviously still reading Nietzsche, and finding him fascinating, and believe it or not, causing me to sometimes laugh out loud. My fan/friend said " This is the kind of poem that could start huge conversations about society as a whole, but also about how we perceive ourselves, how we perceive others and vice-versa... philosophy... gotta love it"...

Yes ain't that the truth... if I hadn't gone into show biz... and all that it entails, I would have studied this subject for sure.

Read on, and I will leave you with your thoughts.

Amoral

Morality is a hindrance,
On the road to forbidden pleasures.
Exposing dark secrets,
Beneath hidden treasure.

With stones in her shoes,
She walks the wild side.
Confession, deliverance,
Will her faith waive

her tide?

The wild one, the mild one,
Slightly off key.
Sweet melodies of youth,
Soaring high, flying free.

No guilt or remorse,
Sailing sensual seas.
Caught up in the warmth
Of orgasmic ecstasy.

Amoral, Amoral,
What does it mean?
To explore the menu,
Of unacceptably obscene?

Amoral, Amoral
Wherever you are.
Amoral, Amoral
Whoever you are.

Happy Hunting!

This is one can that only be described as
PHEW, GLAD THATS OUT OF
MY SYSTEM!!!

There are some things that are just plain hard to bear. They tug at your heartstrings, they frustrate you, they anger you, and they make you cry, but then at some point, you realize the tears have to stop because it will never ever change. The old saying "hope dies last" is true... and the sad thing is... hope eventually does die and THAT is truly sad. I said, "My gloves are off"... my fan/friend replied, "The gloves are definitely off on this one".

Bare knuckled and bare hearted I am leaving the ring. Wait for the bell, and enjoy the fight, and your opponent is 'yourself'!

Ding. (I wonder who will win?)

Elephant In The Room

Oh yes, there it is in plain view,
The elephant in the room.
And, after our meaningless chatter,
Our flower has failed to bloom.
It's about me, and it's about you.
I need to splurge, to vomit.
No more benefit of the doubt.
My gloves are off, no sympathy,
I will tell you what it's all about.
And you can swallow or linger in it.
You're a sorry piece of work,
Full of unfulfilled desires,
You hang on the successful one,
Wanting to burn her in 'your' fire.
And your fantasies jump and jerk.
A lifetime of resentment,
Could it be 'jealousy'??
This word we shall not speak of,
Oh god, what a travesty.
In the end, 'your' discontentment.
I am done stroking your ego
I am done dampening my flame.
I am spreading my wings and flying
No more bullshit, no more game.
We will go wherever we go.
The elephant in the room
Has for me disappeared,
The elephant in the room
Is a big as what you feared.
It's 'your' elephant, it's 'your' doom
My elephant has left the room,
Yours will stay on your shoulders,
my sun shines through your monsoon
Your need is to even the score
You gloom, your doom, YOUR TOMB.
MY ELEPHANT HAS LEFT THE ROOM
Goodbye.

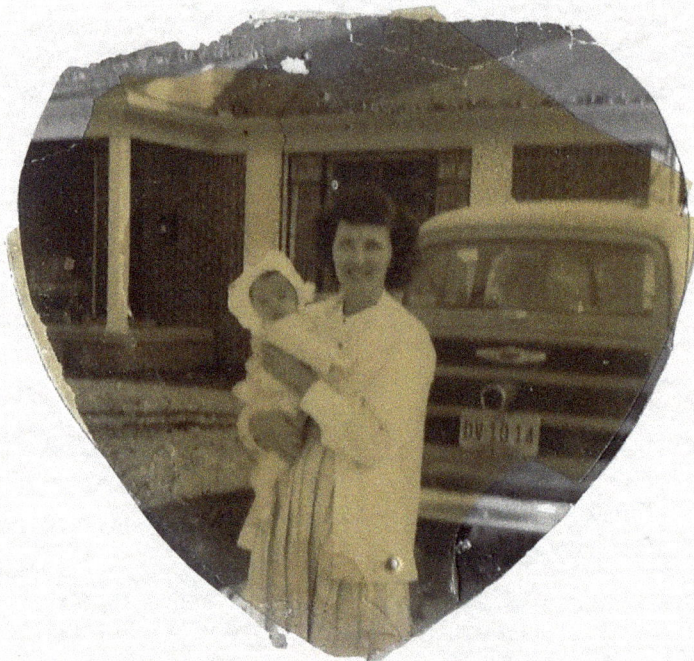

• Me and my mom... 6 months old

The most important person in my life, even though she has been gone since 1992, is my mother. She drives me, she protects me, she corrects me, she understands me, she is on my shoulder every minute of every day. Everyone I know, friends, ex boyfriends, ex husband, fans, family, they always talk about her glowingly.

I finally asked a very good friend of mine,

Why, why why, does everyone talk about her this way... she took a pause and then said,

"Your mother was the most decent woman I ever knew"... Amen... RJP mom... singing with angels... I love you so much... may your influence remain with me for the rest of my days, until its my turn and then, I will join you at choir practice.

My Mom,
My Heart,
Forever

Mom said. never say never.
Not educated school wise,
But oh so wise, life wise.

Mom. always had the answers
To all my questions
To all my whys.

Mom. always made the sunshine

Never say never

Mom... My heart. Forever.

"if you just smile"

Next up... another one that was 'screaming' to get out. These are the ones that really take it out of you because you have to dig so deep and feel things that are better left on the shelf, shoved way at the back where you can't reach them anymore.

Lots of to-ing and fro-ing between my fan/friend and me, lots of questions asked, stanzas queried... I do so love my Q & As, as anyone who has attended one knows.

She asked "When you realise that the status quo is no longer an option and to use your words, you have to 'unload the load' to move forward, I said, "I have never been more content, I think that's what's happened... I have started to see things exactly as they are, I am not swimming against the tide anymore, I am floating on the waves"

Both of us agree on our favourite line, "noisy as only silence can be"

The Least Offensive

A child in need of attention,
Fighting to be heard,
Above the new addition,
Beautiful though she may be.
Lost in shuffling footsteps
Amidst echoing voices,
Above the cacophony
Noisy, as only silence can be.

Cocooned in a safe place,
Hiding her worth deep inside.
Marooned in this secret space,
Orphaned amongst her family.
Escaping on wings of a dream,
Away to distant lands,
Seeking salvation,
Scary though it may seem.

Flying to freedom,
Feet firmly on the ground.
Taking nothing for granted
Not even the peace she's found.
Success rears its head,
She grabs and holds on tight.
Leaving tears on her pillow
Crying long into the night.

Then a partner, and children
In for the long haul, for sure.
But the long haul was too perilous
For one soul to endure.
So, parting became reality
And sides were taken
She hung on to morality
But here beliefs were shaken.

Children do suffer,
Loyalties do fray.
Anger and resentment
And their pain always stays
Is it the sorrow or the failure?
That makes one defensive?
Your child in need of affection,
Is this the least offensive?

Or is it the angry confrontation,
In your second wave of life.
As the patterns keep repeating
Trouble and strife.
One argument, then another
Words fly out, aggressive
A sister, a husband a daughter,
Is this the least offensive?

In the end there is no answer
A conundrum of woes
YOUR heart, YOUR soul.
Is the path you choose,
The least offensive?
Is the end of the road,
The least offensive?
To unload the load,
That's the least offensive.

- *daughter Laura, teenage years, Richard school pic (left)*
  Laura school pic (right) grandma and grandpa Quatro centre.

Giving birth is never easy, and for those of us who cannot do this as nature intended, even more traumatic.

But forever grateful that I was actually able, no matter now difficult, to create, birth and raise 2 children.

That's all that needs to be said. The rest is in the poem.

Born Free

You were trapped inside,
The exit was locked.
Your freedom denied,
Oxygen blocked.

The canal was slim
Too slim to comply.
Yet you pushed and shoved
'detour' read the sign.

Doctor oh doctor,
Give me some release.
I am dying now for sure,
Help me… Please!!!

Danger was near,
There was no choice,
But to cut into my body,
Or lose my voice.

Your voice I had not heard,
Yet I knew it in my heart.
I will love you till my end,
A love that will never depart.

Born free or not,
That is the question.
Let's open the cage,
And relieve our tension.

And so, coming near to the end, three more poems to go.

This next one was written while in Hamburg.

It is an exercise to 'try' and explain why family arguments are so frequent, so painful, and then so easily forgotten.

Its all there folks... read on...

I will be asking questions!!

Blood Binds, Blood Ties

Blood ties,
Unbearable, unbreakable, unshakable.
Deep down inside,
Where we all live.
Unthinkable, generational, and unexplainable
Well, at least I tried.

Blood ties,
Biological, analytical, and irreversible.
No one escapes,
Family whiplash.
Considerable, diabolical, yet understandable.
We all make mistakes.

Blood ties,
Comprehensible, inconsiderable and irrational
Through my veins,
Flow tears of blood.
Psychological, overpowerful, and not extinguishable
Yet, love remains.

Blood ties,
Intolerable, unthinkable, egotistical
We pay the price
In fool's gold.
Unbearable, unbreakable, and irreplaceable
Yes, blood binds.

• 60th birthday Detroit, best friends since age 3 and 4 respectively..
Linda and Susie Kay... and that is a long long time. awwwww

This was earmarked for the last one... I had a sneaking suspicion
that this would be the one, but of course you never know until you're
finished with the book... and as you may guess. It's 'not' the last one..
that comes next. Unexpectedly. My fan/friend said,

"The essence of Suzi Quatro encapsulated in 9 stanzas,
It is the perfect ending"... well fan/friend... nearly the perfect
ending. Guess I wasn't quite done yet.

And so I say anon... never goodbye... I still have so much more to
say!!!

Ode to Suzi Q

Breaking that barrier shoulder first,
Fourth, in a family of five.
When the last of this clan was born,
Mother and child barely survived.
A snub-nosed lonely tomboy,
Scuffed jeans, scuffed shoes, scuffed soul.
Walked slowly through the trenches
Freedom, that was her goal.
Beating bongos to a different beat
Singing songs that no one heard.
She created her own creation,
And became how she preferred.
A hedonistic bass to play on,
In the heat of searching lights.
Hard years of lessons learned
In those rites of passage fights.
Then finally her wings grew strong
And she took her chance on fame.
No matter what price, this sacrifice,
Yes, the world *would* know her name.
And that bell she rang was loud,
It reverberated in her bed.
But her bloodline screamed aloud,
And mangled up her head.
She sailed unchartered seas,
Trailing the blaze of change.
Never pausing for a moment,
To realise it was strange.
She stuck to her guns, unmoving,
Never compromise, never give in.
For to be somebody else's version
Of yourself, is life's biggest sin.
The snub-nosed lonely tomboy
Whose melody remains sweet and true
Scuffed jeans, scuffed shoes, scuffed soul
This is my ODE TO SUZI Q.

And so... after careful deliberation. here is the final poem... written under great duress... as most poems are... this one wallows in the very depths of relationships... and how badly it can hurt when things go wrong. This came out of an ongoing situation which had gotten to breaking point, and when you are at that breaking point when no light is at the end of the tunnel... you grieve,

Even though it's not over until the fat lady sings!

❣

I hope you have all enjoyed my second offering of glimpses into my heart and soul, which are directly connected with my mind.

And, more important, I hope you have gotten something out of it. (she wrote poetically)

The Meeting

With warm hands
I reached across,
The distance between us.
My aim was true.
My intentions, pure.
The result, Atrocious!

With bouquets of words,
Bravely I crossed,
That valley between us.
I am my mothers' daughter
Though my footsteps may falter,
I prayed they would lead to awareness.

I breathed in such anger
My true meaning was lost.
Submerged in your coldness
My god, what a cost.
My futile attempt,
Drowned in aloneness.

With warm hands
I reached across
The difference between us.
There can be no compromise
With deceit and lies,
It's your choice to be…. Motherless.

www.ingramcontent.com/pod-product-compliance
Lightning Source LLC
Chambersburg PA
CBHW062009150426
42812CB00013BA/2582